MW00614894

Reflect on!

ISBN: 978-1-905787-14-2

Printed by
For The Right Reasons
Printer & Publisher
60 Grant street, Inverness, IV3 8BS
Tel: 01463 718844

For The Right Reasons
Changing lives through Enterprise.

FTRR is a local charity which aims to help people who
have had the courage to quit drugs or alcohol,
through volunteering in our Printing & Publishing
and Re-cycling social enterprises

Preface

I first met my friend, Maggie Gallacher, some seven years ago in the Radiotherapy waiting room at Raigmore Hospital. We were both receiving treatment for breast cancer then.

After Maggie's cancer diagnosis, artwork had been her solace. Writing had been mine.

I attend the Creative Writing group at the Maggie's Centre in Inverness, where I was introduced to Haiku by the group leader, Margot Henderson, poet, story-teller and community artist. At first I used this type of verse, which originated in Japan, to describe scenes. (In Orkney, on the West Coast of Scotland and in the Lake District, I found myself putting pen to paper rather than taking holiday photos!) Then I started to use it to describe thoughts and ideas and to reflect on insights and experiences following my treatment for breast cancer. Earlier this year, when talking about our respective hobbies, Maggie and I decided that we could perhaps combine my Haiku verses and her artwork to produce a booklet. Maggie's sketches included places and buildings she had visited, her recollections of family scenes, all of which were special to her. Our booklet would reflect our experiences, expressed in our individual ways. The booklet could be sold and the money raised would be shared between the Highland Breast Centre and Maggie's Highlands, two places where we had been fortunate to meet so many inspirational people.

And that is how 'Reflect on!' came about! We hope you enjoy dipping into it. We've left some blank pages at the end so you can write down your own verses or do a sketch! If you opt for verse, a Haiku verse has three lines, one with seven syllables and two with five. Whatever you decide, enjoy.

Thank you for helping the work of the Highland Breast Centre and Maggie's Highlands.

Mae Bond and Maggie Gallacher

The Highland Breast Centre opened in 2004. It is a modern, purpose built unit which is located at Raigmore Hospital. Thousands of women are seen annually in the centre and in excess of 260 patients with breast cancer are diagnosed and treated each year.

The dedicated breast team are based in the centre; this team includes Surgeons, Radiologists, Radiographers, Breast Care Nurses, Physiotherapists, Clinic Nurses and Clerical Staff.

The breast team offer a current, modern service and use the latest digital technology for diagnostic and follow-up purposes.

Coping with diagnosis and treatment can be challenging and stressful. The staff are here to help and support patients and their families during treatment and afterwards.

The Highland Breast Centre Team

A time and a place
A space to reflect
A way to get through and smile

Maggie's Highlands is a special place for people with cancer as well as their friends and families. Both Mae and Maggie have had a close relationship with us for quite a while, Maggie's is a place where people are welcome whenever they need us – from just being diagnosed, or undergoing treatment, to post-treatment, recurrence, end of life or in bereavement.

We welcome family and friends, as they are often deeply affected by cancer too. We know that those who love and look after someone with cancer can feel just as frightened, vulnerable and uncertain.

Maggie's is about empowering people to live, through and beyond cancer by our pioneering approach that integrates professional help with a community of support in thoughtfully designed centres, a combination that is proving highly effective in alleviating the emotional distress and practical difficulties that cancer brings. Everything we provide is free of charge, so visitors can feel welcome to access our support for as long as they need it.

One aspect of our programme of support is the Creative Writing group that Mae refers to. Our creative writer, Margot, facilitates this weekly group to encourage people to share their thoughts and feelings in a safe, secure and supported environment with people who have or have had a similar experience of cancer.

Mae and Maggie have shown that there are so many positive aspects of getting through cancer treatment. Their ability to share this so openly and creatively is surely testament to their recovery and determination to encourage others to walk through our door at Maggie's.

Thank you Mae and Maggie.

Carole Bridge
Centre Head / Nurse Consultant
Maggie's Highlands

Infinity of ocean.

Bright sparkling waters.

The journey begins.

Silence is alive with hopes.

Listen quietly.

Soon you'll understand.

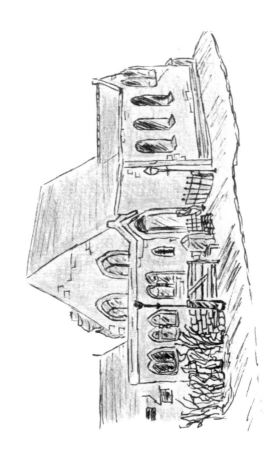

Letting go is hard

but chains of regret

stop the soul moving forward.

Tangled grasses sway,

gracefully moving

as I walk along life's path.

Dawn's pink glow above Black Isle.

Promise of new day.

All's well in my world.

Simple pleasures but most gain

from that which is dear

to the soul alone.

Moonlit steps of liquid gold

invite me to cross

from this world to yours.

Holidays with friends.

Sunshine and good food.

What more is there to ask for?

Child and adult lasts

tell of Thirties' thrift

and hard lessons learned for life.

Such music moves me to tears.

Its beauty stirs me

with restless longing.

Blossom petals flutter down,

carpeting the earth.

Pink and white delight.

A peedie island

with a heart greater

than you can ever dream of.

If Crisis arrives,

then consider this:

threat or opportunity?

I am living life fully

when I am conscious

of each moment's worth.

Waves rushing shorewards

make me long to join

in life's ebb and flow again.

Blue skies, blossom and songbirds.

Senses are heightened

In Spring's splendid days.

Loved ones with us in spirit

keep memories fresh

and sad thoughts at bay.

Avian acrobatics,

as tiny birds play

on Pampas grasses.

All regret lives in the past.

Accept its lessons

and live the present.

Two old shooting-brakes

recall youthful days

and aimless meanderings.

Broom at river's edge.

Sky-blue water flowing fast.

Perfect springtime day.

Social media warp time?

Is the present past

before it is lived?

Old friends will greet us

and make us welcome.

The joy of our island trips!

A flat green island

atop azure seas.

Unlimited horizons.

True companionship:

when silence need not be filled

in friends' company.

Buttercup meadows

awash with pure gold.

Let's stroll through Summertime's joys!

Have you changed at all?

Have you moved with time?

Have you realised your dreams?

After travel's adventures,

friends and family

draw us gently home.

Wild geese on the wing

under puff-ball clouds;

one day I shall fly again.

A bittersweet river walk.

Only memory

as my companion.

Fear is a four letter word.

When you are ready,

write courage instead.

Birdies : eagle, albatross;

captured in language

to enhance a sport.

Three lilac shells on the shore

remind me gently

of our life's beauty.

Dolphins play out in the Firth

and I long to share

their world of secrets.

Time flows inexorably

from past to future.

Live in the present.

Memories are kind again

when each moment lived

brings self-fulfilment.

An Teallach beckons

across narrowed blue waters.

Twilight mysteries.

Sunshine through an open door

invites me escape

the darkness within.

Two sisters sweetly singing

remind of times past,

now forever gone.

Warm summer days stretch

to far horizons.

All's still possible in life.

Age-old agony:

living beyond those

we wish to hold ever close.

All seasons have sunshine days.

Enjoy golden times

whenever you can.

How can you let love help you?

Just ask the question

and see what happens!

Look up at the night-time sky.

Admire moon and stars

before Dawn awakes.

A stone with no names inscribed

guards a peaceful loch.

Forebears' legacy.

The mirror reflects my gaze

and there in my eyes

is my mother's smile.

Crock of gold at rainbow's end.

Closer than you think.

Look within to find.

Dawn's light reflected in pools.

The shoreline awakes

in morning's beauty.

Rainbows arch the Firth.

Mirror imaging.

Nature's beauty reflected.

Snakes teach us lessons.
Let's shed our worn skins
to re-create who we are!

The past and future

are mere descriptions.

The present is what we live.

When you seek answers,

remember others.

You don't need to search alone.

Poppies sway in fields

under leaden skies.

Their warmth brightens up the day.

All experience
must be used wisely
or it may inhibit growth.

Warm flagstones welcome.

Silence draws us in.

What are we going to find?

Cloud shadows chase hillside sheep.

Who will outrun whom?

Upland fun and games!

Sunshine through transparent leaves

glows for me alone.

A wonderful sight.

Be still and listen

to what is around.

Do you hear more than before?

Heavy sand slows me,

giving me more time

to hear the waves' new stories.

Cascading colours

welcome us into

another gardener's world.

Your life may be in your hands,

but you can permit

others to support.

Whenever a change occurs,

it is another

of life's adventures.

A large friendly moon

holds my tearful gaze.

I smile back and he moves on.

Water gives us life?

Here on the west coast,

does that mean eternity?

Tap-tapping gulls on the grass

invite me to join

in life's mimicry.

All our walks must end,

where and when unknown.

The love we shared will live on.

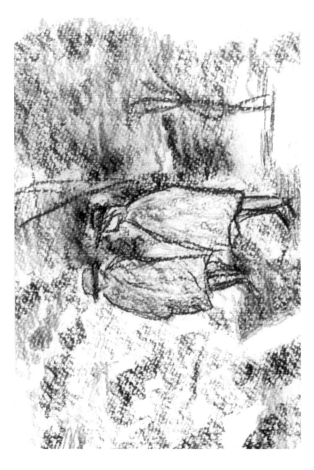

Don't always look for logic.

Sometimes things just are.

Understanding comes.

The sand underfoot,

warm and comforting.

A simple stroll restores calm.

Long cuttlefish clouds

above blue waters,

pointing to infinity.

Dialogue, not monologue.

Doctor and patient:

healthy partnership.

Sunlight beckons me outside

and I will accept

life's invitation.

Relentless waves pound the rocks;

change is happening

which we can't yet see.

Forsake cameras!

You'll remember more

simply being in this place.

Epiphany strikes

when least expected.

Absorb all the new insights.

Moonlight above Borrowdale.

Glistening grey slates.

Lakeland welcomes me.

Waves rushing to shore

make me sense life's urgency.

Make the most of time.

Huge golden moon above Nigg,

half hidden by cloud,

its beauty still whole.

Let memories heal

the aching void left

when we part from those we love.

Home by CHRISTMAS

The present is what we have.

Use it as a gift

to be shared wisely.

Stars in the night sky

send their light to us

that we may follow their path.

The heron stands on the shore.

A still silhouette

in dawn's quiet light.

Perfect partnership

when both the mind and body

work in harmony.

Store good memories;

they are life savings

which will never disappoint.

Seven dressed roses.

Can thorns be removed

from all life's situations?

Mountain silhouettes

in the twilight's glow

stir my heart with thoughts of home.

We don't yet have our future,

so for both our sakes,

let us speak gently.

Sunshine on shoreline.

A new day dawning,

bringing opportunities.

Fine strands of light on water.

Promise of sunshine

when dark clouds move on.

Each generation

leaves its own wisdom

imprinted upon our hearts.

On this sunny summer day,

as I sit alone,

love surrounds me still.

Rape fields reflected

in the Firth's waters.

Bold geometric patterns.

Dark, biting insects

in swarm clouds ahead.

The intrepid walker baulks.

The dying season

brings Autumn's glory:

Nature's own pyrotechnics.

Time is telling me 'Move on'.

I set the past free

and sense its relief.

The present is now.

Are you living it

or waiting for the future?

We round the skerries.

The old town still waits.

Homecoming assured at last?

Birds soar in pink-dappled sky.

A sunset moment

to appreciate.

Childhood's days are spent

in memory's glow.

Can we see the future so?

Crescent moon in winter sky

heralds end of day

and night's welcome rest.

Remember it's love

which causes memories' shards

to surface and sting.

Mist covered mountains
lie hidden beyond our gaze,
waiting to be seen.

Rest follows activity.

Without such balance,

our best eludes us.

Gulls swoop to greet me.

Shrill cries fill the air.

This beach always draws me home.

Who is it I see?

My parent or me?

Have we merged in life's mirror?

Nature causes change.

There is a pattern.

Can you read it correctly?

Sit and gaze around.

Cathedral stillness

quietens a busy mind.

Secret journeys to the heart

reveal much treasure

when life is well-lived.

Green grass cradles curled brown leaves.

Living and dying:

Nature's harmony.

A hush fills the void.

The birds have all gone.

Nature's power is unleashed.

Bare twisted branches

imprint autumn sky

before the deep winter sleep.

Your words give insight.

Spoken or written,

they reveal your very life.

Viewed from another angle,

the mundane takes on

its own harsh beauty.

First fearful moments of flight

and then the delight

of new horizons.

I am transported

by garden magic

to plant and flower heaven.

Colours are fading
but warmth still exudes.
Time cannot diminish love.

Twinkling lights across the Firth

beckon me over

with welcoming warmth.

Solace may be found

in friends' company

or in quiet reflection.

A shadow of cloud

darkens the hillside.

A strange beast roams the landscape.

Procrastination:
thief of productivity
and living life's dreams.

If memories are box files,

open happy ones

to live life fully!

Thundering waves crash

remorselessly down.

Sea reclaims its captive shores.

Circumstance may imprison

our body and mind.

Reflect, then be free.

Choose a good mind-set
to get the best out of life.
Your body hears thoughts.

Autumnal colours,

heather-swathed hillsides.

This is why I have come home.

Looking for needles?

Where are the haystacks?

Can we find them in hay bales?

Old trees arch the lane.

Their foliage still protects

from the elements.

View adversity

as a useful tool

to build strength of character.

The welcome of old

at our journey's end.

Bonds of friendship unbroken.

On welcome currents of air,

gulls soar in blue skies.

Stillness in motion.

Your dreams are Destiny's bridge.

Enjoy, then fulfil.

Life's riches await.

Firth's sparkling waters.

Haze on horizon.

Today promises so much.

Don't wear sorrow as a shield.

Use it as a key

to unlock the heart.

Old memories stir

when I see moonlight

dancing on St Catherine's.

Past generations

whisper their secrets

and sigh for the life long gone.

I long for night's rest

to enjoy my dreams

of the long journey back home.

Elephants, giraffes.

Fantastic cloud shapes

make my day a happy one.

Leafless trees in gentle breeze;

skeletal outlines

let me see beyond.

All choices are mine.

But how do I choose?

What responsibility!

Mist-covered lochs hide themselves

from the tourist's lens.

Beauty uncaptured.

A stone on a stone

to mark I've been here.

Tears flow for unknown heroes.

Semi-visible,

dark slivers of land

reach out to pulsating seas.

A heron's effortless flight

through this silent glen

fills me with wonder.

This is my garden,

planted with much love

to grow future hopes and dreams.

Dark isles rise from deep sea lochs,

mists unravelling

as pale sun shines through.

No more smiles or hugs;

these exist now only in

memory's treasure.

Distant memories

lie on the far horizon,

yet touch my heart still.

Graceful water-lilies float

on sky-blue water.

Perfect reflection.

Friends will move away,

following their dreams

and we, too, must follow ours.

Moonlight ripples dance

on the black water

as I look out from the shore.

Grey November days

heighten anticipation

of December's joys.

I'm a conglomeration

of Heaven knows what

in physical form

A frosty winter landscape

may chill my body

but never my heart.

For the time being,

enjoy our old walks

until you find your own path.

An archway of trees.

Architectural fusion.

Nature and Gothic.

A house can tell us so much.

The creaks and whispers

relate its stories.

Life's like a jigsaw puzzle?

Fit the right pieces,

all's well with our world!

The waves break gently
along the shoreline.
The sea has found peace at last.

Swirling mists and silver tarns.

The still winter world

quietens the soul.

Blue sky, peach clouds, bare branches.

Winter morning dawns

with New Year's promise.

New Year's Day '14.

I promise to make

each single second special.

Winter cedes to Spring.

The cycle re-starts.

Renewal of life's seasons.

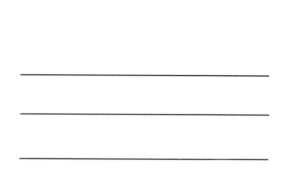